Kathryn, A Missouri Girl

Kathryn, A Missouri Girl

KAY TIMBERLAKE BRYANT

Kathryn, A Missouri Girl

Copyright © 2019 by Kay Timberlake Bryant. All rights reserved.

No part of this publication may be reproduced, stored in a retrieval system or transmitted in any way by any means, electronic, mechanical, photocopy, recording or otherwise without the prior permission of the author except as provided by USA copyright law.

The opinions expressed by the author are not necessarily those of URLink Print and Media.

1603 Capitol Ave., Suite 310 Cheyenne, Wyoming USA 82001
1-888-980-6523 | admin@urlinkpublishing.com

URLink Print and Media is committed to excellence in the publishing industry.

Book design copyright © 2019 by URLink Print and Media. All rights reserved.

Published in the United States of America

ISBN 978-1-64367-609-8 (Paperback)
ISBN 978-1-64367-608-1 (Digital)

18.08.19

Contents

1. Grandmother, the Songbook and Heaven...... 7
2. 56 Cousins and Gooseberry Pie 16
3. Grandfather, Mother and Me 24
4. Persimmons and Paw-paws 32
5. Christmas, Bonnie Bess and Tiny Girl 40
6. Elocution, Rex and the Perm 47
7. Events and Surprises 56
8. Double Digits, a Watch and a House 65
9. Fifth Grade Diary 73

Grandmother, the Songbook and Heaven

Odessa, Missouri in 1918 had a population of 1800, was located about 35 miles south of Kansas City and was a small farming community. It was also home to a six year old girl named Ida Kathryn VanMeter. Everyone called her Kathryn. Now Kathryn's father, Isaac, was the youngest of 13 children who were all married and had children of their own, except for one brother, Joseph, who died at age 19. Most of the others still lived in Odessa or on farms around Odessa. Isaac used to tell Kathryn, "I always say hello to everyone I meet, because I never know when I might run into another VanMeter." Isaac, Kathryn, Kathryn's brother Rex, and Kathryn's mother Minnie, lived in town because Isaac owned a feed store. Minnie was active in the First Baptist Church and everyone knew Isaac and Minnie. Kathryn said "hello" to everyone also.

"Today is a special day because mother and I are going to the farm to see my grandparents," Kathryn said to her doll. "We've been going out to see them several times a week as grandmother is sick. Mother and I ride out in the buggy a few miles to the farm where they live. Their farm house is pretty and, in another month, there will be beautiful colored flowers all around the house. Grandfather is always happy and full of the joy of living. He enjoys his friends, his fishing, the beauty of nature and his family." Grandmother loves flowers, thought Kathryn, especially sweet peas, zinnias and peonies. She is usually very cheerful and always has a special treat for me when I come to visit.

"Something yummy," she says, "I made just for you."

"Grandmother," I say, "you didn't have to do that, but I'm glad you did." Then we laugh. But today, there are no treats because grandmother is sick in bed and I'm feeling sad for her.

Grandmother's name is Ida Belle Smith Rex and grandfather's name is Elgin Oscar Rex. Mother is the oldest of three children. Her brother Archie is several years younger and lives with his family in

Colorado and her sister Pearl is ten years younger and lives in Colton, California where she is the Colton City Treasurer. Grandfather would tell Rex and me stories of the Rex family and how their ancestors had come from France. My father told us the VanMeter ancestors were from Holland. I've just learned that the word "ancestor" means one of your relatives who lived a long time ago. Anyway, mother stayed with grandmother in her bedroom and they visited and I went to the barn to be with my grandfather. He always has stories to tell me. Grandfather reads a lot. He loves books and he knows about places far away across the ocean.

Grandfather said, "Polly-Kate (his special name for me was short for Pollyanna and a nickname for Kathryn) today I'm going to tell you my story." I settled down on a bale of hay with my legs crossed like an Indian and my head resting in my hands all ready to listen. "I was born in Ashland, Ohio in 1857. When I was about your age my family moved to a farm near Lexington, Missouri where your grandmother and I first lived when we were married. I was 22 years old when we got married and we moved to this farm where we've lived for 39 years. So, this was your mother's home before she married your father.

Your grandmother and I were charter members of the Odessa Baptist Church. Do you know what a charter member is?" I shook my head no. "A charter member is one of the first members of the church, people who were members when the church first started. And, I'm proud Polly-Kate that you are one of the current members of the church." I took his hand, smiled and looked up at his strong face, "I love you grandfather."

We walked hand in hand back to the house to get something to eat. My mother had brought some leftover chicken which we had for lunch along with some oranges and cherries right off the tree, and oatmeal cookies mother had made earlier.

"Grandmother, whose house is this?" I asked holding up a picture of a small two-story house.

"Why, that was the house I was born in," she said. Then she perked up and with tears in her eyes, she said "I have a little rhyme I made up years ago about that house:

I remember, I remember the house where I was born.

The little window where the sun came peeping in at morn."

"Oh grandmother," I said, clapping my hands, "that was swell. It reminds me of the rhyming things I say when I jump rope." Grandmother smiled and patted me on the head and asked to go back to her bed.

Soon, it was time to go and I went in and kissed my grandmother on the cheek and told her I loved her and kissed my grandfather good-by too. Mother didn't talk much on the way back home and she looked real worried. Grandfather kept his farm but he and grandmother moved to a beautiful big house in Odessa so grandmother would be closer to mother and to the doctors. Uncle Archie and Aunt Pearl came to see my grandparents right after they bought the house in town.

One month after my grandparents moved to town, grandmother died. I've never known anyone who died. My other grandparents died before I was born. I was very sad and I cried and cried, but not around my mother. I tried to be brave around my mother because I didn't want to make her feel worse. The man, who owned the General Goods Store in town, gave me a bottle of beads because he thought my grandmother was a special person and he knew I was sad. I shall always treasure that bottle. After the funeral, I asked mother, "Will grandmother go to heaven?"

"Yes, Kathryn. Grandmother loved Jesus and she gave her life to Jesus a long time ago. She let Him be in charge of her life and she was a wonderful Christian woman." So, I know Heaven is a wonderful place because my grandmother will be there and I can see her again. Hallelujah!

Grandfather came to have dinner with us several nights a week and would stay and play games with us. Our family loves to play games in the evening and I think playing games helps grandfather to not be so lonely for grandmother. We shoot marbles, play Rook or dominoes or all three. One night grandfather said he'd made a game, a new game for us to play. "It's a lot of fun," he said. He'd taken a piece of wood and put hooks on it and written numbers under the hooks. Then he'd brought rubber rings out of canning jars and he showed us how to throw the rubber rings and try to land on a hook. "Whoever gets the most points wins," he said. Rex won. That's my favorite game now.

Some nights mother gets out our favorite songbook. It's a songbook that teaches values. One of my favorite songs starts with "Be careful little feet where you take me to" and as I sing it, I drop pennies in a jar. Many of the songs are songs I also sing at church on Sunday mornings. I love singing these value songs because I am just learning to read so I can't read the Bible yet, but I learn things about Jesus and about the way He wants me to live from these songs. I think Rex and I are very lucky that our mother and father make sure we spend a lot of time together doing family things.

Sometimes I help mother make pies, cookies or other food dishes in the evenings for people from the church who are in need. Mother usually visits them and brings some food. She is very thoughtful of other people. Someone told me once, "Your mother is always available to lend a helping hand." I want to be like mother when I grow up. But first I have to learn to read.

Ida Belle Smith Rex's house she was born in.

Grandmother Ida Belle Smith Rex

56 Cousins and Gooseberry Pie

"You know, I have 56 cousins," Kathryn announced to her best friends, Julia Schall and Fonnie Wakeman. The girls were lounging under a large Weeping Willow tree in Kathryn's spacious back yard on a warm, sunny day in July, planning their next adventure.

"That's no surprise, said Julia, with all the VanMeters that live around here. Why you can't walk down Main Street without running into a VanMeter."

They all giggled and Kathryn said, "I only told you that because we're having a big family reunion on Saturday and I'm real excited about going."

"How many people do you think will be there," asked Sophie.

"My mother says maybe 70-80 people," said Kathryn. Fonnie and Julia wanted to know all about such a large reunion. They had never been to a family reunion.

"Why don't you both come over again on Monday afternoon and I'll tell you all about it – everything," offered Kathryn.

"Ok," they both replied with enthusiasm.

"And then we can go get a root beer," said Julia.

Being good friends with Julia certainly had its' rewards, thought Kathryn who absolutely loved going to Schall's Drugs which was owned by Julia's father. Not only was it the best place to go for a root beer, it was the only soda fountain in town and Kathryn loved the beautiful marble countertop and sitting on the tall stools that swiveled.

Kathryn could hardly sleep on Friday night she was so excited about the family reunion. She was very curious about meeting 56 cousins. She couldn't imagine so many children being her cousins. She only had 3 cousins on her mother's side, Uncle Archie and Aunt Lena's children: the twins Elgin and Milton and Roma Lee, the youngest.

"Oh, mother, what is that yummy smell?" asked Kathryn as she entered the kitchen early Saturday morning, yawning and stretching her arms.

Mother smiled and answered, "It's Gooseberry Pie. I'm making two of them for today."

"What is Gooseberry Pie? It sounds awful and what is it made from? Surely not from a goose," laughed Kathryn.

"No dear, gooseberries are a fruit and it happens to be my very favorite pie and I know you will like it. In a little while I'll let you taste it and you can tell me what you think," mother replied.

As Kathryn walked back to her bedroom to get dressed she thought about the gooseberry pie and the only good thing she could think about it was that it smelled yummy cooking. Maybe she could tell mother it smelled good and then she wouldn't have to taste it. Slipping out of her nightgown, Kathryn was eager to get dressed for the reunion but knew it was too early, so she just jumped into her favorite baggy pants for now. She was to help her mother load up the picnic basket and today was actually a test. She made out the list herself of everything to go into the basket and then mother would check over the list to make sure everything was included. She reviewed the list now, again, as she didn't want to disappoint mother: napkins, plates, eating utensils, glasses, and the two gooseberry pies. Oh, and we can't forget the big jug of lemonade. She made her bed and set out her new dress mother had made. It was a navy blue cotton dress with white trim around the cuffs and hem and a white belt with navy trim. She then bounded down the stairs for breakfast with her list.

When she reached the kitchen, Rex and her father were already seated at the table. Kathryn scooted into her chair just in time for grace. "Father, for what we are about to partake of we give thee thanks. We also ask your blessing on our family gathering today. We ask this in Jesus precious name. Amen," said Isaac. Father's prayers were always a little short. Mother's were always a little long.

Kathryn started to eat her oatmeal and noticed a small amount of something strange on her plate with the toast. "What is this?" she asked.

"It's a taste of gooseberry pie," said mother proudly.

"Oh," whispered Kathryn with no enthusiasm. She ate her cereal slowly and drank her orange juice slowly, asked for more orange juice and drank it slowly and nibbled at her toast, avoiding the gooseberry pie.

"Kathryn, please don't dawdle, we have lots to do this morning," said mother. So, with a very small forkful of gooseberry pie in one hand and half a glass of orange juice in the other, Kathryn was ready to quickly taste and wash it down. Gooseberries are pinkish in color and actually very sweet. To Kathryn's delight she discovered she really liked the gooseberry taste and asked mother for just a little bit more. In later years, Kathryn would tell people her favorite pie was gooseberry pie. Sometimes it's good to try new things.

Finally it was time to go and Kathryn was the first one out the door. Mainly, she was looking forward to seeing her cousin Margie who lived in Warrensburg, Missouri. Margie and Kathryn were like sisters and since neither one of them had a sister, they were very close and loved being together which wasn't very often.

When we got to the park, there were people everywhere. Mother took the basket and pies and me to where the ladies were gathered. I couldn't believe my eyes. There was more food than I have ever seen anywhere: all kinds of sliced meat, fried chicken, cheeses, fruits, vegetables, beans, sweet potato dishes, potato salad, fruit salads, cakes and pies. And all the ladies were talking excitedly about all the different food dishes. I was introduced, kissed, patted on the head and told to run along. I ran off to find Margie.

"Kathryn, over here," yelled Margie. She and I squealed when we saw each other and hugged. I grabbed her hand and we skipped off to join a group of girls jumping rope, most of whom I knew from school. There are lots of VanMeter kids at Odessa school. Today, there were kids everywhere and all ages: little ones that tugged on their mommy's dresses, teens that were in clusters of boys and clusters of girls, giggling, and some younger boys playing baseball. We lined up for jump rope and they were chanting one of my favorite rhymes.

> Ladybug, ladybug, turn around
> Ladybug, ladybug, touch the ground
> Ladybug, ladybug, shine your shoes
> Ladybug, ladybug, read the news
> Ladybug, ladybug, how old are you?
> One, two, three, four. . . . . . .

There were about 16 girls jumping rope so we visited, exchanged names, laughed and had a good time. It was all quite busy. Then the bell rang and it was time to eat. Tablecloths had been set out on all the tables and all that food was miraculously on the tables and everyone lined up and went along and filled their plates. That took a long time. Margie, her brothers, Earl and Clarence, and her father, Uncle John sat with our family. Margie's mother had died recently. When Margie, Earl, Clarence and Uncle John came to Odessa from Warrensburg they would spend the night at our house. So, Margie and I knew we would be up late tonight talking and sharing all kinds of secrets.

It was fun watching my mother and father chatting and laughing with their friends. Rex also seemed to be having a good time. I was happy because my family was happy. I made sure to get a piece of gooseberry pie for dessert. By the time we loaded up to go home, I'd met my cousins and had some new friends and could hardly wait until the next reunion. 56 cousins is a lot of cousins and I think that is real special. What a wonderful, glorious day. And, Margie is spending the night.

Rex, Elgin, Kathryn, Milton, Roma Lee (cousins)

Grandfather, Mother and Me

"You mean you'll go to school every day with Rex and me and come home about the same time," Kathryn asked her mother.

"Yes, there will be very few differences in our lives," mother said. "While you're at school, I'll be at school, the same school. It will be a new adventure for us." Minnie VanMeter hadn't taught school for ten years in order to be at home with Rex and Kathryn. But she and Isaac had talked and decided Minnie would go back to teaching school. She was going to teach fourth grade. Rex was going into sixth grade and Kathryn was going into second grade.

Minnie asked Kathryn if she'd like to hear the story about her first year of teaching. "Yes, I'd like that very much," replied Kathryn.

"The school I taught in was a one room school and the children who came were all different ages. My first year I had nineteen children from ages six to fifteen. They all had their own lesson programs that they were on and I had lots of papers to grade. Your grandfather gave me a big white horse that I named Jim and I rode him every day to teach school. I had to go early to build a fire in the stove at the school house. The year was 1900 and I was 19 years old. I still lived on your grandparent's farm, helping them on the farm, and Aunt Pearl still lived there also because she was only nine. Uncle Archie was in college. It was very important to your grandfather that I go to college, even though it was very unusual for a woman at that time to go to college, especially someone from a farm. So, I went two years to a teacher college."

"And someday I hope you will go to college as well. Part of the reason I'm going to teach school now is to make sure you get to go to college also."

"Mother, do you have a picture of Jim?" I asked.

"Yes, of course, you can keep it in your room if you'd like," said mother as she came and handed me the picture.

"Mother, you and Jim both look so handsome," Kathryn said smiling.

Mother laughed as she kissed me and tucked me into bed, saying "Well I certainly hope I look more handsome than Jim!"

Two weeks later when grandfather joined us for dinner, I got another surprise and not a very pleasant one. Grandfather said, "Rex and Kathryn, I'm going to be moving away from Odessa to a state called Florida which is way over on the Atlantic Ocean. Here, I brought a map to show you where we are now and where I will be."

I started crying and tried to keep my tears from showing, but soon they were running down my face. "But grandfather, I can't bear for you to not be living so close and coming for dinner and to play games," I blurted out.

He put his arm around me and said softly, "Kathryn, I understand, but twice a year, in the fall and, in the spring I will come and live with you at your house and we'll be together every day then. Would you like that?"

Still sniffling, I nodded my head yes.

Grandfather continued. "Your Aunt Pearl and I are going to do some traveling and I'll get to go fishing every day when I'm in Florida and I will send you post cards with pictures of the places where we travel and you can keep them in a scrapbook if you'd like. There's so much beauty in the United States that I haven't seen and I'd like to do that before it's too late. It's always been a dream for me, a goal of mine."

I forced a smile because I did want my grandfather to be happy and I knew how lonely he'd been without grandmother. "Grandfather, will you still be here for my birthday?" I asked carefully.

"Of course," he replied, and he gave me one of his big warm smiles. School started and I really liked my new teacher. We had some new children in our class and I knew second grade would be even more fun than first because now I could read. Each morning, we all three got up, dressed at the same time, had breakfast together and fixed lunches together to take to school.

Other children in the school came up and said, "Oh, it's so wonderful that your mother is teaching school." She was very well liked in the fourth grade and I was very proud of her.

Soon it was October 5 and my seventh birthday. I had been counting the days for two weeks. Mother had fixed a special dinner for me and decorated the table and made a beautiful cake with seven candles on it. In addition to Julia and Fonnie, mother had invited Sophie Husman and Blanche Schooley to come for the celebration as well. Fonnie's father was a doctor, my doctor actually. Sophie's father owned the mortuary and the furniture store and Blanche's father owner the drug store where we got medicine. When they all arrived I was practically jumping for joy. We had dinner, they sang "Happy Birthday" to me and then it was time for the presents.

We all went into the parlor and there were so many gifts I didn't know where to start. The first gift was a bottle of cologne from Julia. Then a scarf from Fonnie which she and her mother had knitted, some note cards from Blanche which she had decorated herself and a bookmark which Sophie had made with a picture of the two of us on it. "These are all such special gifts. Thank you and I like them very much, "I exclaimed enthusiastically.

Then I opened Grandfather's gift. The card said, "This one is just for you," Polly-Kate, love, Grandfather." I couldn't believe my eyes. I was holding a brand new Brownie Camera that was all mine. I rushed over and hugged grandfather and said, "Oh thank you, thank you. Now I can take pictures and send them to you."

"Yes, dear, I hope you will. That's why I got you a camera all your own," grandfather said tenderly.

Lastly, I opened the gift from mother and father. Mother said, "Your gift is in the card." When I opened the card it read "A gift of piano lessons is being given to you. May you enjoy and let it be a blessing to you and others, love, mother and father."

"Oh this is so exciting," I blurted out as I rushed to hug mother and father. "Finally I get to take piano lessons like Rex and soon I can play the value songs on the piano," I joyfully added.

"Well, that will take a little practice and it's something you'll need to do every day," commented mother. "But I think you're old enough for that commitment." Sometimes, mother had the last word.

It was getting late and we had school the next day so as everyone was leaving, I hugged them all and said, "Thank you so much for coming and making this a special birthday."

But, before grandfather left I asked him, "Is there film in the camera?"

"Yes, of course," he answered.

"Then I'd like a picture of you and me together that I can keep in a frame in my room to look at every day while you are gone," I said taking his hand. Grandfather squeezed my hand and mother took the picture. Then I took some pictures of everyone and so I had my first picture taking experience.

Grandfather left two weeks later and we had a big farewell dinner for him. I gave him a picture of our family which was taken with the camera he gave me. "Here grandfather, you can keep this one in your room and look at it everyday."

He placed me on his knee and said, "Yes, that's a good idea because you know I'll be thinking of you every day." I gave him a big smile and a hug, something I'll miss.

Mother had given me a diary to write in everyday and I usually wrote in it right after saying my prayers. Tonight I wrote: I'll always remember being seven: mother went back to teaching school, grandfather moved away and I started piano lessons.

Grandfather, Elgin Oscar Rex

Persimmons and Paw-paws

"Kathryn dear, please hurry," called mother. "Rex and I are waiting to go pick the persimmons." Kathryn was just finishing dressing when her mother called, unable to decide whether to wear the blue and yellow daisy dress or the baggy pants. She settled on the baggy pants and rushed to join Rex and her mother. Picking persimmons and paw-paws was a special time they all looked forward to.

Kathryn loved to sing the Paw-paw Song which her mother had taught to her and Rex. And, usually she sang it as they were doing the picking. Rex, being 3 ½ years older than Kathryn felt he was much too old to be singing a paw-paw song. But, Kathryn, at age 7, was delighted to sing.

Where, oh where, oh where is Susie?

CHORUS: Picking up paw-paws; put 'em in a basket

Where, oh where, oh where is Susie?
Picking up paw-paws; put 'em in a basket
Where, oh where, oh where is Susie?
Picking up paw-paws, put 'em in a basket
Way down yonder in the paw-paw patch
Way down yonder in the paw-paw patch
Come along, boys, and let's go find her
Come along, boys, and let's go find her
Come along, boys, and let's go find her
Way down yonder in the pawpaw patch

Sing Chorus again

Kathryn would change the last line frequently just to make the song more fun. She'd sing, "Here comes a chicken out of the hatch," or "I'm going to carry a real big batch".

Minnie Rex Van Meter loved to be with her children in the outdoors. She had been an outdoorswoman all her life, having been raised and worked on a farm. She worked a lot with her father, especially with the planting. There were no stores so Minnie and her family had to grow all their own fruits and vegetables. Things like cucumbers, tomatoes, green beans, peas, sweet potatoes, red potatoes, carrots, lettuce, and corn were foods Minnie knew all about – when to plant, how to plant, how and when to water. They also grew pumpkins and watermelons and had fruit trees with apricots, oranges, apples, plums and figs. And, there were so many flowers. Minnie was fond of peonies and zinnias like her mother had been. She knew all of this before she was 7 years old. But now, that her family lived in the city, she wanted Rex and Kathryn to learn about planting and growing also and to be able to identify and name various flowers, fruits, vegetables and nuts.

Today was persimmon day. They would also pick paw-paws and walnuts. Persimmons are a sweet fruit when picked at the right time and Kathryn and Rex would eat almost as many as they picked, while Minnie would take them home and make Persimmon pudding and Persimmon jam. It was quite a walk to get to the woods where the Persimmon trees were fresh for the picking. And the paw-paws were nearby. Kathryn, Rex and Minnie each carried two baskets – one for the paw-paws and one for the persimmons.

And, as it was late October, it was also a little chilly, so they walked fast. Thank goodness there was no wind.

Part of walking to the meadows to pick persimmons and paw-paws was seeing and greeting the people you knew along the way. Kathryn's friend, Fonnie, lived on the way and, Kathryn was hoping she would join them for the picking and was looking forward to seeing her dear friend. When Kathryn had asked Fonnie the day before to join them on this excursion, she'd said, "Stop by on your way to the woods. I'm sure it will be all right with my mother." Kathryn and Fonnie loved to be together even if it was just talking. They would talk for hours about anything that came to mind and both Kathryn and Fonnie loved to go for walks. They'd walk to town to get a root beer soda at Schall's Drug Store, or walk to other friends' houses, or just around town.

"Fonnie, Fonnie, hi; so, can you go with us to pick persimmons and paw-paws?" asked Kathryn excitedly.

"Sure. I'm all ready to go," she said, as she marched down the front step swinging a wicker basket with a big smile on her face. They walked briskly a few more blocks and finally reached the woods. The sun shining, combined with the bright and varied colors of fall leaves, made for a visually stimulating walk. The woods with the thick trees and colorful bushes of autumn, plus the golden color of abundant ragweed, added to the beautiful picture. This was the best time of the year to be in the woods.

"All right," mother said. "Just remember don't eat any persimmons until we get home. I don't want any belly aches tonight and I also need to count out the persimmons for pudding and jam before you can eat any."

Kathryn was a little disappointed as she always enjoyed eating at least one persimmon while picking the rest. So, she said to Fonnie, "Let's sing the paw-paw song and pick them first. I know we can eat one of them while we are picking." So, off they went singing and skipping and swinging their baskets.

Now paw-paws are not as pretty as persimmons or as big. They're speckled, splotchy and the riper they get, the uglier they get. And, once picked they only last for several days, so pawpaw lovers find 'em, wash 'em and eat 'em, spitting seeds all the way. Kathryn and Fonnie were both very proper young ladies, but they liked being able to spit out the seeds when no one was around watching.

Paw-paws are yellow and sweet with the flavor of mango, banana and pineapple and are great to eat right off the tree.

Kathryn's father Isaac would, when he wasn't too busy at the store, make Paw-paw Ice Cream. Oh, that was really yummy and Rex and Kathryn were always available to help when their father would say, "Today is Paw-paw Ice Cream Day." And, of course, Minnie, a schoolteacher, made sure the children knew that a paw-paw had 3 times as much vitamin C as an apple.

In no time at all, the baskets were full. Rex had chosen to stay with Minnie and helped her pick a lot of persimmons. Kathryn and Fonnie had a few persimmons and a lot of paw-paws. "We'll pick walnuts another day," said Minnie. "Our baskets are full now and we'll give some to Fonnie's mother on our way back" And, since it was several hours before dinner, Minnie let Kathryn stay and play with Fonnie. Minnie promised Kathryn she could have a persimmon for dinner.

And Minnie smiled as she and Rex walked past the front gate hearing Kathryn say, "I love persimmon and paw-paw days."

Kathryn's mother, Minnie, when
she was about 19 years old

Minnie and her horse Jim

Christmas, Bonnie Bess and Tiny Girl

Only three more weeks until Christmas and 7 year old Kathryn and 10 ½ year old Rex were pretty excited. They had already made out their Christmas lists, or at least made sure that Father and Mother knew what they were particularly interested in. Rex wanted a tool box, gloves and a new sweater. Kathryn wanted a rubber doll, which was the latest rage, a new sled and a set of doll dishes. But she'd be happy with any surprise that someone gave to her.

Tonight was the big Christmas party at the First Baptist Church in Odessa and most of Kathryn's friends attended this church so they would be there. There was a huge Christmas tree which her father, Isaac, and some other men had cut down in the woods and transported to the church. Mother and some of her friends had decorated it. They would be going to church for dinner, a program and then, Santa and the Christmas gifts.

Mother had made Kathryn a beautiful new red taffeta dress for this Christmas event. It had a nice crinkly sound to it, a pretty little standup collar and little taffeta ruffles at the bottom of the hem and sleeves. Kathryn also had a locket to wear that her Aunt Pearl had given her when grandmother had died. Inside the locket were tiny little pictures of her grandmother and grandfather. She was singing every Christmas carol she could remember while she was getting dressed. Her favorite was, "Deck the halls with boughs of holly, fa-la-la-la-la-la-la-la-la . . .

"Kathryn, time to go," yelled Rex. Why was he always dressed before she was?

"I'm coming," she hastily replied as she ran to the front door. Mother and father looked very nice as mother had on a pretty new print dress with lots of red in it and father was wearing a suit. Rex was wearing trousers, a shirt and a vest. Mother had made some divinity candy which was her favorite sweet treat to make at Christmas and she made it in all different flavors and colors. It was always delicious.

When they arrived, Fonnie called out to her, "Kathryn, over here."

Kathryn asked if they could sit with Fonnie's family for the dinner and mother said, "Ok." The girls immediately told each other how much they liked the dresses they were wearing and talked about other Christmas activities, especially the Christmas program coming up at school where both girls were singing in the chorus. Dinner was wonderful – turkey, mashed potatoes, gravy, stuffing, cranberry muffins, creamed corn, sliced carrots, sweet potatoes mixed with brown sugar, and a wonderful assortment of Christmas cookies and candy for dessert, including mother's colorful and tasty divinity candy.

After dinner, the choir director led them all in singing Christmas carols and then the lights went dim. Suddenly we heard, "Ho, ho, ho, merry Christmas." And, Santa appeared. He was very jolly and plump and he had a huge bag loaded with gifts. He asked if we had all been good and we all nodded yes. Then, he started pulling out gifts and calling out names. "Rex VanMeter," he called and Rex smiled and went up and got his gift with a thank you. His gift, I noticed, was a new pair of warm gloves and he seemed happy. Finally, I heard the name Kathryn VanMeter and I smiled and received my gift with a thank you. When I opened it, there was a tiny set of doll dishes and I was very pleased and thankful. I smiled at my mother.

After the program, each child received a bag of candies for Christmas. I was pleased to see Tootsie rolls individually wrapped, a stick of Wrigley's Chewing gum and a stick of the new Chickley's chewing gum, a piece of divinity (I know where that came from), life savers, Necco wafers, some taffy and other assorted hard penny candies.

The Christmas program went very well at school and I enjoyed singing in the chorus. The program was actually a pageant about the first Christmas and Jesus in the Manger, and all the different grades were able to sing songs. I hope maybe next year I can have one of the speaking parts. Mother, father and Rex were there and many other VanMeters because lots of VanMeters were in the Christmas program. Afterwards, we had punch and cookies. It was a fun evening and we all chatted about it on our way home.

Rex and I had saved up our allowances and bought mother and father a box of chocolates called Whitman's Sampler. We got it at Schall's Drugs and hoped mother and father would find it to be a special treat. I also took a picture of Rex with my Brownie camera from grandfather and had him take a picture of me and we made frames for the pictures to give them along with the chocolates.

Of course, Christmas Eve I couldn't sleep. I was just like the children in Moore's, Twas the Night before Christmas, with visions of Christmas passing through my mind. Well, the next thing I knew the sun was shining and it was time to get up. Into the parlor Rex and I bounded, after waking mother and father.

Mother said, "Let's read the Christmas story from Luke, remember that this holiday is all about Jesus and pray. We did, although I must admit I was a little bit fidgety. Then we opened each gift, one at a time. That's fun because it makes opening gifts last a lot longer. Rex got a new tool box; all the more special because father had made it for him and he got a beautiful new blue sweater that mother had knitted for him. I did get a rubber doll and a red sled so I was thrilled. Mother and father seemed quite pleased with the chocolates from Whitman's and they really liked our pictures. But the only gift from grandfather was a card.

After breakfast, mother and I started making some pies in the kitchen. Today, we were making mincemeat and pecan pies to take to our cousin's house for Christmas dinner. While we were making pies there was a knock at the door. Rex and I ran to see who it was. There was a man we'd never seen before with two small puppies. "Are you Rex and Kathryn VanMeter he asked?"

"Yes," we both replied at the same time.

"Well, Merry Christmas," he said and handed us each a puppy. The puppies were Boston Terriers and they each had a card around their neck.

The card said, "Merry Christmas. Take care of these little ones and give them lots of love, from Grandfather and Aunt Pearl."

Mother told us the dogs were pedigree dogs and the first ones in Odessa. I didn't care what they were, I was just happy that they came from grandfather. Mother said we could each name one. Rex named one Tiny Girl and I named one Bonnie Bess. Later when we'd calmed down, Rex and I asked, "What are pedigree dogs?" Mother said they are from a specific breed of dogs that have been registered and they are pure Boston terrier dogs. They sure are cute. Then we wanted to know where they would sleep, what they would eat, how to hold them and take care of them. Mother said, "I think Bonnie Bess and Tiny Girl are tired. Let's let them rest on a rug in the pantry for a while." Rex and I were excited to be going to see our relatives for dinner but we would have gladly stayed with Tiny Girl and Bonnie Bess instead.

That night I said, "Thank you Lord for such a special Christmas and for such a wonderful family."

Elocution, Rex and the Perm

Some interesting things happened in our family after I turned eight. Mother went on a train to Kansas City to have her hair "done," which was something she never did. When she came home and walked into the kitchen where the rest of us were gathered, we were all speechless. Mother had curls all over her head and she'd never had curls before. She smiled at our stunned looks and said with a twinkle in her eye, "this is called a perm. I'm the first woman in Odessa to get a perm and it cost $1.00 a curl."

I looked at Rex and he looked at me and we decided not to ask mother how many curls she had. Father said, "It looks quite nice and you look very stylish." Rex and I smiled at mother and shook our heads in agreement. From that time on, mother got several perms a year. Perms became very popular in Odessa.

One of mother's friends told her she was a real "trend setter." I asked her what that meant and she said, "Someone who tries something different first before everyone else." I'm proud of mother being a trend setter.

Rex was almost 11 ½ years old and he'd been asking mother and father repeatedly what he could do to make some money. Finally, one May day after school, mother sat down with Rex and talked to him about some ways he could make money. His first money-making adventure was selling rabbits. He discovered very quickly that raising and selling rabbits were two very different things. Raising rabbits proved to be very difficult and time consuming. Father helped Rex build a rabbit hutch to raise the rabbits in and father also took Rex to buy four rabbits – 1 male and 3 females for mating. Although Rex had read in the newspaper that selling rabbits was becoming a popular business, obviously some important details had been left out. Rex was soon spending hours on his rabbits: feeding and buying the feed, watering, cleaning out their hutches and nests, breeding and overall management, as well as trying to get people interested in buying the rabbits. By the middle of summer, he'd finally sold all his rabbits and was eager to move on to something else. We never even had a pet rabbit after that.

So mother and Rex sat down again and talked about another money-making venture for Rex. Eskimo Pies were brand new in the United States in 1920 and everyone loved them. So Rex decided to sell Eskimo Pies and put together an ice cream wagon of sorts. Actually, selling Eskimo Pies was a little easier than selling rabbits and definitely more fun. Besides you didn't have to talk people into buying what you were selling - everyone liked Eskimo Pies. When Schall's Drugs started selling Eskimo Pies, Rex stopped selling them and that was the end of the Eskimo Pie selling venture. However, he at least made a little money.

Then it was time for school to start and Rex and father agreed that next summer he would work at the feed store to make money. Rex, trying to be very grown up, said, "Well it was a learning experience." Yes, it was one for me too and I decided right then and there that I would never have money-making projects.

Rex and I usually were up early on school days because one or both of us would be practicing the piano before going to school and the other would practice after school.

Rex asked mother and father if he could take saxophone lessons instead of piano lessons.

This was the year Rex seemed to want to try new things. But, he was quite interested in the saxophone and seemed so serious in learning to play, that mother and father agreed.

I was quite glad because now I could practice piano every morning, by myself, and not have to think about it after school. I tried to be out of the house when Rex first started practicing the saxophone – the sound was very irritating. But he soon improved and was actually quite good on the saxophone. He was so excited because next year he could play in the school band. He would be the only saxophone player in the band.

However, mother had a new plan for me after school. "Kathryn, a teacher friend of mine is coming today to talk to you and me about Elocution Classes," said mother.

"What's that?" I asked.

"Elocution is defined as the art of effective public speaking," mother informed me. Mother was an avid reader and always kept herself informed of what was going on in the world, especially in the field of education.

Actually, it sounded kind of interesting to me, so I said, "ok." Miss Somers came after school and showed us a book titled Delsarte Recitation Book. She said this was the best book for elocution and was first published in 1889.

First she told us the incredible true story of Francois Delsarte of whom it was said, "this master possesses a method so perfect, a style so pure, a passion so profound, that there is none in all art so noble or divine." (Steele Mackaye) By now I was eagerly waiting to hear more because the story of Francois Delsarte started when he was a young child; poor, alone and starving to death. Miss Somers continued telling us that a voice with moving power back of it can make all the difference in a presentation. Maybe mother had told her I really wanted to be in the school Christmas Pageant. I don't know why this woman thought I was interested in speaking in a voice with moving power and expression. But, I continued to listen. First, she read us a recitation called "Her Answer" about a young man proposing to a young woman. She almost made these people real as she was reading this tale.

Then she said to me, "do you know "A Dutch Lullaby" about Wynken, Blynken and Nod?"

"Oh yes," I answered.

"Would you like to read it with me?" she asked with a smile.

"Sure," I responded.

And so, we first read it together. Then she asked me what this reading was about and what was being said. We talked about that and she talked about the lines where there was a lot of emotion and then she asked me to read the first verse by myself. This was my first recitation:

Wynken, Blynken and Nod one night

Sailed off in a wooden shoe:

Sailed on a river of misty light

into a sea of dew.

"Where are you going

and what do you wish?"

The old woman asked the three.

"We have come to fish for the herring fish

that live in this beautiful sea,

Nets of silver and gold have we,"

said Wynken, Blynken and Nod.

    She told me I read very well and my enunciation was quite good. I knew about enunciation because mother had worked with me when I was younger to pronounce very distinctly A-E-I-O-U.

    Miss Somers said, "I'll leave this book with you and you practice reading to yourself and then out loud. Each time you read to yourself, ask yourself what is being said and how would you say the same thing if it were you." That was the beginning of my elocution classes and, like mother; I guess I was a trend setter, because no other girls in Odessa were taking elocution classes at that time.

Kathryn and Rex

Rex and Kathryn

Events and Surprises

Another new adventure happened to me the year I entered 4th grade: mother was my teacher. We had a long talk about this before school started so I would know exactly what was and wasn't expected of me in class. But still, it was a little unusual for your own mother to be your teacher for a whole year. So far, we are both doing just fine.

1920 was an eventful year with many firsts. Grandfather came again and stayed until after my birthday and one night while he was still with us, he took us to the new and only movie theater in Odessa to see Mary Pickford in Pollyanna. This was the first movie for our family to see, although grandfather had seen movies in Florida. "Kathryn, you will particularly enjoy this movie because you will meet little Pollyanna and you will understand why I nicknamed you "Polly-Kate."

The movie was "swell" and I took grandfather's hand as we were leaving the theater and said, "I'm glad you gave me that nickname because I like Pollyanna and her attitude." He squeezed my hand. I really liked the word "attitude" and used it whenever appropriate.

Afterwards we walked to Schall's Drugs and the whole family had sodas. When we got back home, grandfather said I have a surprise for all of you and he pulled out five candy bars from his pocket, one for each of us. These are called Baby Ruth candy bars. They are brand new, delicious and I brought them with me from Florida. We all decided they were definitely delicious and a new favorite treat for us. I saved my candy wrapper so I could give it to Julia Schall and she could ask her dad to get some for his store.

The next major event for me was getting ready for the Christmas Pageant and I finally had a speaking part (probably I should give credit to Miss Somers and my elocution classes). I was actually to play the part of Mary and mother made my costume and helped me learn my lines. It was the second Saturday in November and grandfather had to leave the day before, so mother and I were practicing my lines. Rex and father had left earlier to run an errand.

Mother kept looking at her watch and then suddenly said, "Let's go out on the front porch and practice your lines." I grabbed my coat, prepared to do as she asked but wondering why we were going out in the cold when it was nice and warm inside. We got to the front porch and one of many new cars in Odessa was coming down the street with the horn honking.

It stopped in front of our house and father and Rex jumped out all smiles. Mother hurried down the stairs and I followed as father said, "here she is, our first car ever and a brand new one." We were all so excited as we opened doors, got in and out, sat in different seats, investigated the back, admired the curtains that you could attach if it was raining, honked the horn again and father showed us how to drive it. Then we all went for a drive around the block, my first time in a car. This car was a 1920 Overland and the second most popular car being produced in America behind the Ford. It cost about $500. I've never seen my father so happy. 1920 was a year they called a boom year for automobiles and everyone seemed to be getting one. Father and mother said the automobile would change the course of history forever.

The night finally arrived for the Christmas Pageant, the same week as our wonderful Christmas Dinner Program at the First Baptist Church. So that was a very busy week. In addition, mother was making many batches of her now famous divinity candy. The past two years I helped her a lot with the divinity and actually made some batches all by myself. I was a little nervous for the Christmas Pageant, but calmed myself down because I knew my lines really well. There were so many people in the audience and most of them I think I knew. But all went well and I enjoyed it. I'll have to tell Miss Somers there was "power in my talk." She'll appreciate that. Father and mother said they were very proud of me. That meant the most to me.

The next new event happened the night of the Christmas Dinner Program at the church. When the bags of candy were passed out, we were told by the lady in charge, there was a new kind of candy in our sacks. She held up a sample and said this is the very first Christmas season ever for the candy cane. We all pulled ours out of our sacks and instantly decided to try it. It was real "swell." (Aunt Pearl asked me once what "swell" meant and I told her it meant wonderful. She started using the word all the time after that). That was the beginning of a new Christmas holiday tradition. People even hung candy canes on their trees and that year Schall's Drugs had candy canes during the Christmas season and they also had Baby Ruth candy bars. Thank goodness.

Mother came back from town one day with three books she had bought: Pollyanna for me, a book on saxophones for Rex, and a book for herself. Mother read her Bible and the newspaper every day. I really hadn't seen her read too many books.

"Mother, is that a special book you got?" I asked.

"Yes," she said, "It's a best seller."

"What's that?" I asked.

"A bestseller is a book that's the number one most popular book being read in the country and this book is by a well-known author named Zane Grey. The title of the book is The Man of the Forest. Your father might enjoy it also."

After Christmas and a major snow storm, we had some relatively mild days. Friday evening while we were playing Rook, father and mother announced that the next day we would be driving the Overland to Warrensburg to see Uncle John, Clarence, Earl and Margie.

Rex and I were so excited that we spilled all the cards on the floor when we jumped up from the table. "Will we spend the night?" I asked.

"Yes, we will," smiled mother. Warrensburg is a college town and Uncle John owned a barber shop and a large house near the shop where he rented rooms out to college students. Warrensburg is about thirty miles from Odessa and, before we had the Overland, it had always seemed like a very long trip.

"Mother, can I go to Schall's drugs and get some candy canes and Baby Ruth bars to take to Warrensburg?" asked Kathryn eagerly. Mother said, "They might be all out of candy canes because everyone was buying them at Christmas. But, you can try." I was able to get both.

The next day as I jostled along in the back seat of the Overland, looking at the scenery, I thought about all the new events this year: mother was my teacher, went to my first movie, candy canes and Baby Ruth candy bars were introduced, we had our first car, we were on our first road trip, mother got the first perm in Odessa and I finally got a speaking part in the school Christmas Pageant.

It was a happy day I thought as we were on our way to see my favorite cousin, Margie. "Mother, now that we have the Overland, will we be able to drive to Warrensburg more frequently?"

"Yes, we definitely will and we have lots of other places we can also go to because, now, we can get there quicker."

"I must take a picture of me and the Overland to send to grandfather and tell him that now, like him, we will be able to see more of the world," Kathryn said proudly.

Kathryn and her family's first
automobile, 1920 Overland

Kathryn's 4th grade class with her mother, Minnie, who was the teacher and Kathryn next to her

Double Digits, a Watch and a House

One rainy September evening I was in my room, looking at the calendar, and counting the days to my tenth birthday, when mother came in and said, "Kathryn, it's time for dinner and we have a special surprise for you and Rex."

I moved quickly to the kitchen table, where Rex and I sat eagerly. Of course, since it was the fall season, grandfather was with us. Father smiled at mother and grandfather, looked at us and said, with a twinkle in his eye (father always had a twinkle in his eye when he had a surprise, a joke, or something funny to say), "We're moving to a big new house in two weeks. It's one of the largest houses in Odessa and the only one with an inside bathroom. There is a barn, a chicken house and a big pasture next door." Rex and I got very excited and had lots of questions. Father held up his hands and replied, "One at a time, please."

Rex wanted to know about the downstairs. "Well, father continued, the downstairs has a large parlor, a large entryway, a large kitchen and a dining room. There is a front staircase when you walk in the front door going to the second floor and a back staircase from the kitchen that goes to the second-floor hallway.

Quickly I asked, "What's upstairs and where is the bathroom?"

"The upstairs has three bedrooms and the bathroom," replied father.

"You mean we don't ever have to go outside to an out house again?" I asked, quite amazed.

"That's right," said father.

Two weeks later we moved into our new big house, which quickly became "home" to me. Soon all the neighbor kids were coming to our house to play outside because the big pasture next door became the playground where all the kids came. Ten days later, I asked mother, "Can Fonnie and Sophie spend the night, Friday night?"

My friends liked our new house too and my bedroom was so much larger than the one in the old house, that there was enough room to have girl friends spend the night. Mother agreed and suggested that maybe Fonnie and Sophie would like to spend the night after my birthday party. It was agreed and soon my attention turned to becoming ten years old, finally I would be double digits. It was wonderful to be able to eat our supper and dinner meals in the dining room instead of the kitchen. Mother liked the arrangement much better also. I still had to help wash and put away the dishes, but at least I wasn't looking at them while I was eating.

This year we decided to make my birthday party a Halloween Party as well. So, everyone came in costume, even grandfather. Rex and father didn't wear costumes, they said, because they were in charge of the games. Rex, father, and grandfather had decorated the pasture to look like a cemetery and they would blindfold people and take them by the hand through the cemetery, making spooky noises. They had decorated the inside of the barn where we bobbed for apples, sang some silly songs and played grandfather's game of throwing the jar lids on the hooks. Fortunately, Rex didn't play or he would have won. Fonnie won this time. Mother told a spooky Halloween story and then we went inside the house for cake, punch, candy and to open gifts. Then, of course, Fonnie and Sophie spent the night and we stayed up and talked and giggled to quite late. Then grandfather left for Florida.

Our family created a lot of fun memories in our new home very quickly and I tried to write down most of them in my diary. Spring came and went; as did grandfather, but before he left I told him proudly that I had my first summer job. I would be working in a canning factory, canning tomatoes and I would make $40 for the summer. "That's wonderful, he said. If you put your money in the bank, I'll buy you a watch." That was certainly worth putting $40 in the bank. Kathryn didn't know of any other girl in school who had a watch. Summer went by quickly and Kathryn thought a lot about the watch.

The summer ended, as did the canning job and mother told Kathryn, "I've contacted your cousin, Clarence, who's now working in a jewelry store in Kansas City and he's sending out two watches for you to choose from. Grandfather wants to make sure you choose the watch you want." I could hardly sit still I was so excited.

Every day, after school, I would look to see if the watches had been delivered. It seemed to me it was taking a long time. Then mother came in breathless from the barn one afternoon after school, carrying a package that had been torn with wrapping paper and string falling off and said, "Well, Kathryn I think Bonnie Bess and Tiny Girl got to the package before we did. But the watches haven't been damaged." Quickly, I finished ripping open the boxes and the two watches. One was round and the other one was oblong. I liked the round one the best. I put it on immediately and went to my room to write a thank you note to grandfather. I also learned that putting your money in the bank is a smart thing to do and can be very rewarding.

I wore the watch from grandfather every day. It was doubly special because the brand of the watch was Elgin, which, of course was grandfather's name. I tried to have Rex take a picture of the watch to send to grandfather and decided he would just have to see it the next time he came. From that time one, any money I earned, I always put most of it in the bank. But, whenever, we went outside to play in the pasture, I took the watch off and kept it on my dresser. I had a special little pink crystal box that Aunt Pearl had given me and I kept the watch from grandfather in that.

Grandfather and I continue to write letters to each other in-between his visits and I continue to write in my diary. I am still enjoying my piano lessons and sometimes get to play in a recital. Now I am old enough to really enjoy the programs at the church on Sunday evenings for the young people. Mother is still teaching fourth grade. I'm still in fifth grade and Rex is a freshman in high school and is still playing the saxophone. Even so, we still play games as a family in the evenings, although not so much, because Rex works after school at the feed store with father and then he has to do his homework in the evening after dinner. We entertain often in our lovely new home because we have so much more room and we have lots of relatives. Holidays and family reunions are still special because of all our relatives and Margie and I get to see each other frequently because Uncle John and father both have cars and the drive back and forth is easy. It's a good life and I'm happy.

Epilogue: Two years later Kathryn lost the watch and was almost sick because she was so upset at losing this watch from her grandfather. She was totally devastated. Her father bought her a new watch, but it wasn't the same. One day some time later a workman was digging up the ground on a path that Kathryn had previously walked. He found the watch with the name VanMeter on the back. When he saw the VanMeter name, he asked Kathryn's father if he knew of anyone who had lost a watch. So, Kathryn got her watch back. And, sometime she might ask you, "Have I told you my watch story?"

The house Kathryn called "home" where she lived from age 10 until she left for college

Fifth Grade Diary

1922

February 24, Saturday

This morning I got up at 5:30 and helped my mother and brother get ready to go to Kansas City. Then I went to my cousins to spend the day. I had a good time there and one of the things I did was to pop a basketful of popcorn. I went to the train station to meet my mother and brother at 5:30 in the evening. They brought me a bobby comb, string of beads, ribbon and marbles. I am very happy.

Good night

February 25, Sunday

I got up late today. After breakfast I studied my Sunday school lesson. Then I went to Sunday school and church. I had a cold and I stayed at home the rest of the day. I was lonely and felt bad because I could not play out of doors or go anywhere. So I must say good night. I am tired.

February 26, Monday

This morning I was sick and didn't feel like studying my lessons or practicing my music

Every time I'd start to read or write my eyes would water and I had a bad cold. I wanted to go to the picture show but mother said no so I got my lessons. Mother said I could go when I wasn't sick.

Good night. I am tired

February 27, Tuesday

I still don't feel good but I went to school just the same. Today in arithmetic I was on 14's and I missed one so will be on them tomorrow. I hope I will get off it. Miss Powell said in language for us to write a composition on What I Expect to Do Saturday. I don't know what to say yet. But I will know in the morning. Today Kenneth, Elmer and Wilmon got a slapping and had to stand on the floor. This morning Miss Broyles told us about the class of Kindergarten she taught. We had writing today. We gave a little play named Betsy Ross and George Washington. We are going to give it again tomorrow.

Good night. I am very, very sleepy

February 28, Wednesday

Dear Diary: I haven't any lessons to get tonight and so it seems awfully lonesome to me. This evening Mrs. Keenan called up and told mother a secret and mother said she wouldn't tell me till tomorrow. I wish I hadn't been home when she called so I wouldn't' have known anything about it. I am anxious for tomorrow to come. This evening after school mother went uptown so I went down to daddy's store. There were lots of people down there. And he was very busy. When I came home my cousin Ruby came down. The ditching has been on this street and is through and is now caving in. Ruby said I sure would laugh if you fell in it and just then it caved in with me. Of course I felt like a monkey and the best thing about it, it didn't hurt me. Well I haven't anymore to say.

Good night. I am tired and ready to go to bed.

March 1, Thursday

Dear Diary: This morning I practiced my music lesson. Rex and I both wanted to practice at once. So mother said the first one dressed would practice. Rex was through first. Today in arithmetic I was on my fifteen's but I got off. Tomorrow I will be on my sixteen's. This evening I went up to daddy's store and I had a good time.

I am sleepy. Good night.

March 2, Friday

Dear Diary: This morning I got up early and practiced my music. Today it rained and I didn't go outdoors. This evening after school I went up to daddy's store. I met Julia Evelyn up town and she was going to have her hair trimmed and she wanted me to go with her. We got some ice cream and then we got some candy. We walked around and then it was time to go home. So we both went home and got our music lessons. I listened over the radio and heard Schenectady, New York and many other stations.

Good bye

March 3, Saturday

Dear Diary: I woke up and the sun wasn't shining and that made me feel bad. I got dinner today because mother didn't feel well. Then we washed the dishes and went down town. Rex and I played marbles down at daddy's store. Just for fun I helped fill some sacks of feed for I didn't have anything else to do. Then I came home and played with one of our neighbor boys. We ate supper and then listened over the radio. I am sleepy and haven't anything else to say so I am going to bed.

Good night.

March 4, Sunday

Dear Diary: This morning I got my Sunday school lesson. Then I ate breakfast and washed and got ready for Sunday school. I played until it was time and then I went to Sunday school and church. Then I came home and made some fruit salad while mother got the rest of the dinner. Then after dinner I read the paper. Then my girlfriend came and we played school and drew and had a good time. She stayed till half past five. We sure did have a good time. Then I went to the B.Y.S.U. (Baptist Youth Student Union) and I took part in it. I did not stay for church because Ruby couldn't and had to come home with her.

Good night.

March 5, Monday

Dear Diary: This morning I got up early and went to school. We had the picture machine in Geography and Miss Broyles gave some of us pictures to tell about. She gave me one and she said we did pretty well. At noon, Miss Broyles called Irene Kite and wanted her to take a package over to Miss Lucy Elliot's. And she asked me to go with her. I've just got home from the fashion show. They had awfully pretty dresses, suits, sweaters and kaki outing suits. There was a great big crowd there. Good night

March 6, Tuesday

This morning when I woke up I was surprised for it had snowed in the night. And so we had a white cover for our bed. By night it was nearly all gone. Well I didn't do much today except get my lessons. This evening after school my cousin came down to play. She stayed till about six and then she went home. Tonight I have been playing school and I was teacher and letting on like I had pupils. I have a good time by myself. I haven't got anybody to play with so I play by myself. I am tired and it's time to go to bed. Good night

March 7, Wednesday

Dear Diary: This morning I went to school and after Hygiene class I took my music lesson. Sophie Lee brought her dinner and we had a good time. After dinner, mother and I went uptown. Mother and I looked at the silks, crepe taffeta dresses for her and me both. Then we came home and Ruby came down. Tonight I have been listening over the radio and been planning what I want to do Easter. I am tired and sleepy. Good night

March 8, Thursday

Dear Diary: Today, I went to school and in arithmetic I was on the seventeen's but tomorrow

I will be on the eighteen's. In spelling I made a hundred. This evening after school I went over to Alice's to play. I stayed till 5:00. We sure did have a good time. Then I came home and Rex and I played marbles. Then I listened over the radio and got my lessons and am sleepy and going to bed. Good night.

March 9, Friday

Dear Diary: Today in arithmetic I was on the eighteen's but did not get off of them. So, will be on them tomorrow. This morning I practiced my music and went to school. I got a hundred in Spelling. Tonight when I came home Rex was sick. The dressmaker is making me a brown taffeta dress. It has lace buttons and a little ornament on the side. Good night

March 10, Saturday

Dear Diary: This morning Rex is worse. I can't practice my music on account it makes too much noise. But I don't care about that. Today I went down town three times to get things for Rex. I listened over the radio. They gave a good program. It was the Star Broadcasting. Good night

---

March 11, Sunday

Dear Diary: This morning I got my Sunday school lesson and got ready to go. I stayed for preaching. I was the only one in my class. So I read a paper all the time. Today it rained pretty hard. Rex is still sick but I think will be alright soon. Good night

---

March 12, Monday

Dear Diary: Today I went to school. It is raining now. Rex is better but is still sick. In arithmetic I am on the eighteen's but didn't get off so will be on them tomorrow. I hope I get off. This evening after school I went up town. It was raining then. Good bye

March 13, Tuesday

Dear Diary: This evening after school mother and I went up town. I went down to see about my hat but it wasn't done. I stayed up town a little longer and then came home. I wrote two letters today one to my grandpa and the other to Aunt Pearl. Well I can't think of anything else. So Good night

---

March 14, Wednesday

Dear Diary: Today is the day for Rex and me to take our music lessons. But Rex has been sick and didn't get to practice and neither did I because the piano was in the room he was. So I won't get to take my music. Today in arithmetic I was on the eighteen's. And I guess I never will get off. I will be on them tomorrow again. I listened over the radio and got my lessons. Good bye

March 15, Thursday

Dear Diary: today it rained very hard. At noon Miss Down came in and said that those that had their lunch go in the 6th grade and eat. The others had to study. We got out at 2:00. I came home and painted the rest of the evening. In arithmetic I was on the eighteen's but missed two so will be on them tomorrow. Goodnight

---

March 16, Friday

Dear Diary: Today it is pretty. Miss Powell is reading us a good book. The name is "Rebecca of Sunnybrook Farm." This evening I sure was glad it was Friday because I don't like to go to school. Today in arithmetic I was on the eighteen's and I got off. SO Monday I will be on the nineteen's. Good bye

March 17, Saturday

Dear Diary: This morning I woke and it was awfully pretty. I always feel like working when it is pretty and not gloomy. This evening I went down town but didn't stay long. I thought well tomorrow I guess will be pretty. I baked some cakes and pies this morning. Good bye

---

March 18, Sunday

Dear Diary: As usual this morning I got my Sunday school lesson. Then I went to church. After I came home, I read the paper. In the evening I stayed home but read "Heidi" so I wasn't lonesome. Tonight I went to church. Alma Helms was there and we sat together. When the lights went out, Mr. Wilkenson went and called up to see when they would be back on. We did lots other things until the lights came on. Good night

March 19, Monday

Dear Diary: Today in arithmetic I was on the nineteen's and got off of them. So tomorrow I'll be on the twenty's. Today it is cold and the wind is blowing hard. I wish it would get pretty so I could wear my slippers. I haven't much to say. Good night

---

March 20, Tuesday

Dear Diary: I will write a few lines. Today I got a letter from Aunt Pearl but I was so disappointed for she didn't say when she was coming home. Today in arithmetic I was on the twenties and tomorrow I will be on the twenty-first. Today on account of examinations we didn't have all of our lessons. Good bye

---

March 21, Wednesday

Dear Diary: Today it is time for me to take my music lesson. I got a card from grandfather and he said he was going to start home next Tuesday. I helped mother a whole lot today. I have an awful toothache. In my Geography test I was above standard. Frank got the highest grad in our grade. Good bye

Baptist Church of Odessa

www.ingramcontent.com/pod-product-compliance
Ingram Content Group UK Ltd.
Pitfield, Milton Keynes, MK11 3LW, UK
UKHW022209230426
12048UKWH00016BA/730